Prague Winter

Books by Richard Katrovas

Poetry

Green Dragons
Snug Harbor
The Public Mirror
The Book of Complaints
Dithyrambs
Prague Winter

Fiction

Prague, USA
Mystic Pig: A Novel of New Orleans

Memoir

The Republic of Burma Shave

Prague Winter

Poems by
Richard Katrovas

Carnegie Mellon University Press
Pittsburgh 2004

Acknowledgments

Grateful acknowledgment is made to the editors of the following publications in which these poems first appeared:

Crazyhorse, Great River Review, Kestrel, Los Angeles Review, New Delta Review, New Orleans Review, Poetry, Poetry Miscellany, Seattle Review, Southern Anthology, Virginia Quarterly Review, and *Washington Square.*

"Elegy for Robert L. Jones," "Love Poem for an Enemy," and "Prague Winter" first appeared in *Poetry.* "The Boxers Embrace" appeared in *Perfect in Their Art: Poems of Boxing From Homer to Ali* (Southern Illinois University Press, 2003). "On the Day After Allen Ginsberg's Death Someone Thinks of Me," "Love Poem for an Enemy," and "The Turn" appeared in *Poets of the New Century* (Godine, 2001). The poems in the section titled *1989* first appeared, sometimes in slightly different form, in *The Book of Complaints* (Carnegie Mellon University Press, 1993).

I thank the editors of *Crazyhorse* for their 1992 Poetry Award, and the Louisiana Endowment for the Arts for a fellowship that allowed me to finish the poems from *1989.* I thank the Fulbright Foundation for a fellowship and an additional grant that first allowed me to travel to Central Europe. I thank Susan Gebhardt, Edward Hirsch, Rodger Kamenetz, Philip Levine and Stanley Plumly for wise council this book may not adequately reflect. I thank, too, my Western Michigan University colleagues Stuart Dybek, Jaimy Gordon and Arnold Johnston for reading the final version of this collection and commenting so thoughtfully.

Book design: Coral Compagnoni & Audrey Whitman

The publication of this book is supported by a grant from the Pennsylvania Council on the Arts.

PENNSYLVANIA
COUNCIL
ON THE
ARTS

Library of Congress Control Number: 2003103590
ISBN 0-88748-405-0
Copyright © 2004 by Richard Katrovas

10 9 8 7 6 5 4 3 2 1

Contents

I   1989

The Bridge of Intellectuals / 11
"Socialism with a Human Face" / 13
After Frank Zappa's Visit to the Castle / 14
St. Vitus / 15
Weekend / 16
The Book of Complaints / 17

II   An Untethering

Rehab / 27
The Dog / 28
The Car, the House / 29
Saint Roch / 30
Second Marriage / 32

III   Tucked

Love Poem for an Enemy / 35
The Boxers Embrace / 36
When Someday the President-Elect of the United States Requests
    That I Compose and Recite a Poem for Her Inauguration, I Shall
    Stand at the Podium and Speak the Following: / 38
Elegy for Robert L. Jones / 40
On the Day After Allen Ginsberg's Death
    Someone Thinks of Me / 42
The Comfort Inn / 44

IV Wind in the Chimney

The Letters / 49
Meluzina / 51
Elegy for Miroslav Holub / 52
In Memory of Miroslav Prochazka, Scholar of Czech Literature / 53
Libuse / 55
Germans in the Pool / 57
An American Lawyer in Olomouc / 59
Tick / 62
Prague Winter / 64

V Feuilletons

The Art of Teaching / 69
The Tennessee Williams Literary Festival / 70
My Best Lesbian Friend / 71
Movie Critics / 72
Pariah / 73
The Art of Revenge / 74
If I Were a Jew / 75
The Gossip / 76
The Cumulative Weight of Despair / 77
Rich People Slumming in Academe / 78
As When Someone with Long Beautiful Hair
   Turns Around / 79
George W. Bush Was Very Nice to Me / 80
Each Customer is an Odious Task / 81
In America They Would Get Shot / 82
The Slovaks / 83
Ordinary Czechs Singing on TV / 84
There's No Tragic Weather Here / 85
The Liberal Arts / 86
The Super Rich Are an Oppressed Minority / 87
Two Fellows Only a Little Swarthier Than I / 88
A Brief History of Your Conception / 89

For Dominika, Ema and Annie

I
1989

The Bridge of Intellectuals

If Crane had been a Czech, and deigned to live
till '53, he might have more than praised
a bridge, for in that year of Stalin's death,
artists and intellectuals of Prague—
but only those the Party had to fix
after an "elegant coup" in '48—
finished their bridge across the Vltava.

Each morning did they bring their lunch in bags?
Did they bitch and curse and clown around behind
the foremen's backs? Were there foremen? Or did
each man (were there women?) pull his weight
unprodded by the ethos of his class?
Of eleven bridges down the spine of Prague
it stands the shabbiest and least necessary.
From the road leaving town one sees the tufts
of grass and weeds muscling through the rusted
transoms that trains, some say, must rarely cross,
and notes the webbed faults in the dark concrete
of columns lifting from the water like
wet khaki pant legs of old fishermen.
To those whose ambitions for bourgeois fame
got them torn from their tasks to labor here,
is there ironic consolation that,
as work is a matter of identity,
so many praised workers remain unnamed?

Anonymous bones of generations lie
the snaking length of China's ancient shyness;
unknown apprentices applied the strokes
that smeared celestial radiance onto cheeks
of lesser angels in the master works.

The petty, silly little men who snapped
the blossom of a generation from
its living vine have watched their own bridge crumble,
and even as this bad joke stands unused,
dilapidated on the edge of town,
perhaps its "rehabilitated" builders—
most dead by now, though some, no doubt, at work,
scattered throughout Prague, in little flats, alone—
feel vindicated in their bitterness,
if bitterness survives absurdity.

I'd like to know that once or twice a year
an old man, whose hands are soft from idle thought,
comes, by bus or car, to gaze awhile
and simply marvel that the thing still stands.

"Socialism with a Human Face"

Several times those dizzying weeks
I wondered aloud if "socialism
with a human face" were not still more
than the sentiment of Dubcek's
wounded generation. One young Czech laughed:
"Socialism doesn't work. Our lives are proof!"

The day after Martin Smid got martyred
only to reappear beaten but alive,
no one knew that tanks and troops would not roll in.
Obcansky Forum, Havel as its heart,
was coalescing in the chants
of the disenfranchised "masses."

In the streets after rallies, a calm mulling
persisted into night, and the Square flickered
where students kept their vigil. I observed them
gathered close, wrapped in blankets, sipping hot drinks
brought by friends, their faces sweetened by
ten thousand candles, and considered
that their lives might never be so pure again.

After Frank Zappa's Visit to the Castle

One may imagine him saying to Zappa,
"I've been a fan since 'Weasels Rip My Flesh.'"
Yet to know he loves his beer and music,
or that years ago he soldered a crazy
Ionesco to his own Bohemian heart,
does not prepare the credulous outsider
for Havel, designer of chic uniforms!

Less than one year out of prison, newly
ascended to the bloodless seat of power,
he looked, it seems, upon his Color Guard
and was, if not offended, deeply bothered
by the cut and colors of what they wore,
and so sat down with pen and drafting paper
and sketched out how the uniform should drape
the smart, svelte soldier, and in what hues of blue.

Bohemians, Moravians, and Slovaks
have rarely marshaled martial acumen.
To see them marching on the Castle grounds,
ceremoniously grave, one might affirm,
though, the prerogative of small nations
to strut absurdly through the rituals
of masculine identity and pride.

There is a quiet courage of irony
which visits the great lovers in a world
antithetical to their dreams of peace,
and no matter his crimes, each prisoner
must know his world by walls and uniforms.

It's not unlikely a troop of Sea Scouts
from Bangor, Maine, or Fresno, California,
would whip the Czechoslovak Color Guard,
yet what mother of invention would not squeal
to see her boy decked out by a president?

St. Vitus

In the great Gothic cathedral of Prague—
designed, of course, to scare shit out of peasants,
and so parlay a huge and abstract doom
into incontrovertible power—
I strolled, nine months after the gentle purge.

A god who dices with the universe
surely will not care for such drab splendor,
but there it stood, dank, crusted with relics,
neither museum nor sanctuary.

The Holy Roman Empire once murmured there,
and Charles IV is kept in the huge cellar.
I bought a ticket and slumped down the steps
with the other tourists, mostly Germans.

Raised in a nation obsessed with beginnings,
I could not stipulate resolution
as the measure of gross identity.
In the foundation of St. Vitus,
large, dirty walls of granite shoulder death,
and I imagined kids through the centuries
screwing in the hollow pockets of rock,

sneaking down, wicked, sweet, full of guilt
yet drawn inexorably to the cool places
near the crypts of kings and bishops, as though
passion justifies what passion hastens.

Weekend

A broad zone from southern Poland
through central-south Moravia
is dying of chemical blight, and no randy hope
of revolutions nor common markets
will make it once more lush and vital.
Eight months after the "people's triumph"
I'd returned to see my child be born.
Swollen to her eighth month, my child's
strong mother hiked with me five k's
to the Polish border, all the while
quizzing: *strom . . . kyticka . . . zeleny . . .*
Our child, she insisted, will speak Czech,
will have a Czech identity.
She paused often to pluck berries,
and spoke with humor of her parents,
divorced for years, still hunting mushrooms
in the same frail woods outside of Prague:
"They live the same lives, do the same things.
One wonders why they separated."
Blight is a matter of degree,
of course, and that ancient forest
of her country was still attractive;
indeed, the sick rains had so thinned it out
it appeared more lovely for all
the delicate angles of fallen trunks,
and for patches of clearing where
stunted shrubs carpeted the ground.

The Book of Complaints

for Pavel Srut

1.

I was told that most
establishments kept
a "Book of Complaints"
for the sour stories
of the poorly served,
the principle being
familiar to patrons
here in the rich West:
the customer is right,
always, and as such
may stride like a god
through a world of aisles,
touching and choosing.
But the "customer"
was, more precisely,
a mere citizen,
a consuming unit
suffering to shuffle
through too many lines
toward barely stocked shelves.
And when she complained
it was to her shoes
as she queued for fruit,
or to the wall by
the kitchen sink as
she emptied of cans
the plastic bag she'd
kept stashed in her purse,
then to the coal-grayed
sky of sumptuous Prague
as she stood at the
window, in autumn,
a righteous restraint
withering within her.

2.

I stood among them,
dumb emissary
of good intentions,
and listened to their
chants and studied their
faces. The autumn
sky would turn to ash
each afternoon in
Wenceslas Square as
the bold crowds swelled, and
the peeved old men in
the Castle got grimmer.
"Dominika, what
is he saying now?"
I would ask again
and again, and my
patient friend would pause
to translate the blared
complaints of that hour's
representative,
explaining nuance
and brief history.
"Richard, you just don't
know what it's like to
live under such liars,"
she said, applauding
another public
sentiment of rage,
applauding her youth
and "socialism
with a human face"
(at least the idea
if not the practice).

The night that Jakes
shuffled from power,
a fine rain drizzled
and kids piled into
cars and hammered horns
and swished Czech flags, and
the faces on trams,
even of the old,
in that gold light shined
with contentment;
the Book of Complaints
seemed, for the moment,
finished.

3.

But it is
never done; like hair
it lengthens after
death as head skin shrinks
and turns to leather.

Dominika, dear
one, beautiful and
bright, everywhere sour
heads, having spent youth
seeking a cure for
fear of death, find in
the death of passion
a bitter solace.
Benevolent, some
would save the whole world
from the body's will,
that half-remembered
dance of the fetus

whose dazzling finish
is each body's first
wailing entry in
The Book of Complaints.

The privileging of
mediocrity
is a sin far worse
than the fratricide
it always inspires.
Dull fathers pull long
faces for the young,
who are not amused,
though learning to laugh
with one's whole body
is the first stage of
a righteous slaying.

Where, before, people
laughed bitterly and
to themselves, or in
small, muted clutches
sucking cigarettes
and quaffing rich beer,
from mid-November
to mid-December
they laughed openly
and infectiously.
It is wonderful
to hear such laughter;
a revolution
of laughter often
it seemed, and Kafka,

squinting up from his
own Book of Complaints
in a cramped chamber
of a gray heaven,
surely felt the bliss
of vindication.

4.

When poor Martin Smid,
the revolution's
martyr for a day—
his purpled, swollen
face a flag of harm—
was thrust on TV
to prove that he lived,
that riot police
had not quite killed him
(as though the thousands
swarming his shrine of
a thousand candles
would casually scatter
at proof that he lived),
fact withered beneath
the putrid fictions
of twenty-one years,
and though it no doubt
hurt his face to laugh,
one can only hope
Smid saw the noble
purpose of his "death,"
and managed to smile.

5.

From the Charles Bridge at
night the Castle shines
in golden floodlights
of ambiguous
glory. Bohemians
stroll the quiet dark,
to my eyes passive,
sighingly pliant.
Yet I am humbled
by the memory
of a dour people
opening their lives
to the world and to
themselves, and chanting
the essential truths
inscribed there, in blood.

To the Old Town Square
the tourists will flock
and yawn up stiff-necked
and still beneath the
Astronomical Clock,
waiting for little
wooden figurines
to spin in their slots,
pirouetting robots
chiming the hour.
Each time I return,
a tablet of Czech
dissolving on my tongue,
I'll stand in the Jewish
Cemetery, among
the shuffled, tilting,
gray, smooth, weathered slabs—
Jews buried ten-deep

signified by mounds—
and think of Loew
inserting the scroll
in his golem's mouth.

On most ragged slabs
are pebbles, each speck
a token, a prayer,
a petrified flower
for the laughing dead.

The revelation,
at first, seems simple:
a "state" is only
the page on which one
inscribes her most bitter,
consistent complaints,
a page filled with ire
scribbled in various
hands, signed boldly, or
left anonymous.
We are the mounting
tallies of each her
discontentedness,
and desire, the un–
inscribable, gets
confounded in the
act of complaining.

6.

I regard a world
that is beautiful
and rank, and couch what
I see in language
that is palpable
and rude, for nothing

marked in the cool light
of managerial
regard survives its
last bitter affront
to the gaseous sky
or sooty windows,
and my heart's complaints
I mean to survive
unto the sweet eyes
of those I have loved
and would wish to love.

Amid the almost
funny tilting slabs—
that cram-packed ghetto
of Prague's lost lovers
tilting as a field
of flowers is ruffled
unevenly by
a randy, swirling,
dank autumnal breeze—
I will bitch a prayer
for Loew's loveless
automaton, and
for each hovering soul
among the muted,
rain-smoothed, pebble-crowned
black headstones, and bitch
prayers for the new life
of Prague, pristine page
onto which real lives
will be written, one
complaint at a time.

II
An Untethering

Rehab

Two springs, I filled our rooms with chirping fleets
of fledglings quiet women of the zoo's
Bird Rehab Center fetched from fallen nests.
My tasks were just to feed them, keep them warm
and shoo away the cats that gathered on
the balcony above our lush courtyard.
Mockers, jays, tough proletarian birds
grew fast and pulsed away; though even as
I brought more tiny eaters home in boxes,
the grown ones gathered every morning, into
summer, on the railing of the balcony
at 6:15 a.m., and squawked until
I stumbled out and dropped a pinch of moist
cat food down each screamer's gullet, to bid
it pop upon the air and disappear.
Then I padded in and fed the babies.

Those were good years in a marriage most would judge
a good one, all in all. We worked hard and laughed
a lot, pursuing separate interests, and came
together every night with no agenda
but the comfort of our coupling, and sleep.

When weak ones shriveled, I grew despondent,
isolating them until they died or
rallied, and when they quit their begging, and when
their hideous small faces—the bulging
monster eyes lidded with veins—dangled back
upon their too-delicate necks, I cupped
them in one hand and stroked them with a finger
until the last perceptible breaths had ceased.

The Dog

As my colleague drives me to work, a brown dog
lopes into the street. A subdued lover of
lost creatures, a woman who lives alone
but for her two infirm beloved mutts,
she swerves and touches her breast, relieved to be
beyond the event horizon of that doom.
She does not look back, and nor, in fact, shall I.
Surely the dazed thing was kept for years and then
rejected, or simply drawn by odors
down long blocks of odors toward the moment,
lost and drunk on all that olfactory wisdom,
he careened onto the blacktop and through
the lives of several lucky drivers, and one
life fated for a morning's inconvenience.

On the pleasant span between the bayou
and the golf course, our conversation veers
from whether unused sick-leave might not count
toward that sixty-percent-of-base-pay bliss
we've both begun to dream of, and whether next
year our Agenda For a Better Way
will win the hearts and minds of frightened colleagues,
and lights awhile upon my sweet ex-wife.
Otherwise vicious in our gossiping,
we are tender, always tender when we speak
of her, of her travails and conquests since
the marriage—always it is "the marriage"—
died, such that all "we" were became a thing
outside of "us," and wanders still the gross
contingencies, the foul and bitter ground
of where it seemed, together, we would go.

The Car, the House

If I were rich, and my blood blue, I'd lay
before your feet dear things and stacks of cash.
My imperial guilt would swell and groan to hand
you all that might sustain a delicate life.
Though you are not delicate, only wronged.
A childless marriage is a luxury,
neither necessary nor advisable,
until age or some great illness lays one out.
Yet tethered so, the coupled heart may tug
against its bond, but if it pulls away . . .
This is just to note, dear, I was a prick,
and an asshole, and every other foul
despicable thing a woman wronged may scream.
As you nickel and dime me, darling, for
a monthly stipend none would say I owe
except perhaps your mother and your lawyer;
as you, sweetheart, unburden me of just
enough to make me wince each month to scrawl
my signature beneath our family name
to which the pinched sum is made payable;
I'm healed, a little, as if by leeches,
and so it seems some ancient cures still hold
their uses, though ancient punishments should be
the choice of one like you, so wronged so long.
Let every woman hurt pick up a stone
against the man who lay down with another!
Let all her friends and family, and even some
of his, ring the deep pit to help her pelt him!
Good woman, beautiful best friend of my youth,
the car, the house are yours; the debts are mine.

Saint Roch

We rented in the Quarter several years,
then bought a modest two-floor wooden house
ten blocks—and worlds—away, on a Ninth Ward street
named for a saint assigned to hear bleak cases,
a goofy street as gay as straight, black as white,
as working-class as new-rich gentrified.
It was a perfect place not to raise a child,
to be an arty couple, youthful but
not young enough to feel that we were young.
And I was superficially happy there,
and must assume she was genuinely so,
for when our marriage fell apart, that is,
when I dismantled it so clumsily,
she seemed a part of her was in a coma.

From the window above the stairs, one could
not help but gaze into the trashy yard
that butted up against our property,
especially when the cackling began.
Almost every day that boy would howl,
rocking violently at the center of
the yard, in the midst of broken pipes, broken
pieces of appliances, and gray planks
strewn over scattered piles of busted bricks.
I call him a boy, but he was over
thirty, and, standing in the rubble,
rocked until it seemed he'd fly
apart. But revved up to his limit, he'd keep
his furious pace for hours, worse than any
bad neighbor's bad dog, and yet we rather
liked him, or the idea of him, and did
not lodge complaint. Yet as the marriage sank

to hell, I couldn't hear his voice and watch
him rocking in a joyful fury and
not feel his ecstasy a mockery.
Almost every day the idiot achieved
a bliss, it seemed, independent of his life,
for how could such a creature know such joy
from rank particulars of such a life?
How could he be so wise and yet so vacant?
So wretched in particulars yet blessed?

Last week I walked my daughters through the church
in Vysehrad, in Prague. The four-year old
was not impressed, but being full of lunch
was quiet in her mild distraction; the ten
year-old chattered rapid-fire inquiries.
Of the numerous gilded figures on the walls
and columns, several saints stared calmly out:
What is a saint? my oldest darling asked.
It is a person who survives great pain
and, preserving faith, does impossible things.
Faith in what? What kinds of impossible things?
I answered as best I could, without faith,
and she seemed satisfied, but then she asked
about each saint, needing details, and I
was stumped by most, but said Saint Roch was charged
by heaven with listening to the sickest lives,
and as I droned on, once more holding forth
to one who is the juicy core of joy
about a subject I know nothing of
but ill-remembered facts, I thought of how
a saint of poorest health may spend his time
alone, in heaven, amid the rubble there.

Second Marriage

I am embarrassed by all my old poems,
as a wise poet said I would someday be.
"Someday" arrived in increments, broken
promises to a dear friend who thought me
wholly incapable of deception,
though in fact lying to her was easy,
even, in some grotesque way, necessary.

When I hold my daughters, the fruits of my
deception; when I tickle them till they
shriek and punch me again and again,
shrieking; when my girls are so
happy they scream and punch me and climb
on me shrieking for more, more tickles, more hugs,
more wrestling on the bed before they sleep;
when my daughters are so alive to all
I am and all they are, the lie of life,
that is, the lie that life is telling for
the moment, is our uncluttered joy,
and though it justifies nothing I have done,
there is nothing sullied it does not cleanse.

III
Tucked

Love Poem for an Enemy

I, as sinned against as sinning,
take small pleasure from the winning
of our decades-long guerrilla war.
For from my job I've wanted more
than victory over one who'd tried
to punish me before he died,
and now, neither of us dead,
we haunt these halls in constant dread
of drifting past the other's life
while long-term memory is rife
with slights that sting like paper cuts.
We've occupied our separate ruts
yet simmered in a single rage.
We've grown absurd in middle age
together, and should seek wisdom now
together, by finishing this row.
I therefore decommission you
as constant flag ship of my rue.
Below the threshold of my hate
you now my good regard may rate.
For I have let my anger pass.
But, while you're down there, kiss my ass.

The Boxers Embrace

In Prague or in New Orleans, my perfect night
of guilty pleasure is to watch a fight.

I know that it is heartless past all speech
to thrill at two men's pain as both must reach

across the bloody billion-year abyss
to strike the other one, or make him miss.

Yet when I gaze upon the frank despair
of spirit-broken people who must bear

the torments of cool fiends they cannot see—
systemic meanness and brutality

of bureaucratic processes that hide
the facts of who has profited and lied—

I see inside the grotesque and plodding dance
of boxers something beautiful: a chance

to mediate the passions of the tribe
by what the ritual of fights describe

(as arm a sudden arc upon the gleam
within that space); for public fights redeem

our sense of being, at once, in and out
of nature, and so map the human route

across the razor's edge of slow extinction.
Such is the truth of all destructive action,

transcending histories of consequence
and serving therefore as a mottled lens

unto the bifurcated human heart
whose one true nature is to break apart

revealing beast and angel wrapping arms
beyond all consequence of temporal harms.

As systems fade, transform, reconstitute,
the fools will blather and the wise stand mute,

then innocence must suffer out of reach,
and over time our best intentions leach

through all the lies we hold as history.
No yearning human heart is ever free,

except when it has found its one true base:
where the last bell rings, and the boxers embrace.

When Someday the President-Elect of the United States Requests That I Compose and Recite a Poem for Her Inauguration, I Shall Stand at the Podium and Speak the Following:

I don't belong here.
This isn't about me,
of course,
but how can I stand before you—
whom it is about,
"it" being the false majesty
of all *this*—
and not feel the genius of democracy
swarm up
out of your inane sweetness?
She whom you have chosen
has appointed me your poet,
your ideal voice for a moment,
and the moment is pregnant.

Let me tell you a little about myself,
because that's all I know how to do.
My narcissism is your narcissism,
and we are therefore truly doomed.

But the odd circumstances of my life
may not be spoken in public;
I shall therefore say simply
that my crimes have been small
if numerous, and each has centered
on the vagaries of desire.

I am doomed in my cynicism,
but will never die, willingly,

for an idea, and in this
am blessed as my children are blessings.
My blessings are therefore wholly of
a different order than yours, which are
the essence of righteousness, which is
in all times a willingness to die for ideas, especially the ones
that only mean the rich require sacrifice.

There is a wisdom of youth
to which one must aspire
and then, upon achieving it, lose.
Perhaps this is why poetry
is dead to formal occasions,
and why therefore there are no
sacrosanct formal occasions
but those issuing from the wisdom of youth,
a condition to which I am happily dead.

Let's gaze into our hearts
and, when we have finished weeping,
resolve never to look again where nature forbids.

It is the lot of humanity to be foolish,
and we, by God, are the most human of the earth,
though our fits of lucidity dazzle
in great blooming bursts
whose crumbling sparks
get tucked between the stars.

Elegy for Robert L. Jones

There was a man so slow
his friends would make their dates
with him two hours earlier
than when he was required.
He spoke and thought, it seemed,
a tick or two behind
his friends, though what he said
was often beautiful.
He would arrive mumbling
apology, and those
who had awaited him
just smiled and shook their heads.
He was so slow the shuffle
of his shoes was like
a rain that's not a rain,
but first, stuttering drops.
He drank his liquor slowly,
too, and every night.
And every night, with each
slow pull on something cold
and cheap his voice dropped
a little more, though his
lucidity did not
diminish; it only stalled
before the morning light.
He wrote such poems of love
a man's respected for
by five or six who read
of love with cold regard.
He wrote them with his heart
in such a way that those
who wince to hear "the heart"
may barely nod, then sigh.
And he wrote them slowly.

One summer night of empty
bottles and much laughter,
some friends heard crashing waves
and dragged him off to swim
past midnight. The grunion
seemed a writhing on the beach,
and lights of traffic and
the stars drew shadows over
him and glittered in the foam.
He swam too slowly, and got
dragged down and trapped by wave
on wave, until his friends
hauled him out of danger.
So it would be for years.
His painfully slow life
would get dragged down, and friends
would pull him to the lip
of some fresh misery.
He lost jobs, wives, money.
But he never lost his friends.
And even as his poems
no longer ooze from him,
and even as his heart—
that lovely aching thing
whose only issue was such
sentiment as cynics loathe—
has ceased to mosey on,
his friends stand astonished
to know he somehow slipped
ahead of all, into
that place where now he sits
and, smiling, waits for them.

On the Day After Allen Ginsberg's Death Someone Thinks of Me

for Gail Wronsky

A woman phones whom I've not seen
in eighteen years, and didn't know
that well. She seems put off a bit
when I don't recognize her name,
but speaks of Charlottesville and folks
we knew in common, for an awkward
minute, until my memory
unclogs and spills forth images.
She called, she says, just to tell me
she remembers a party where
I punched some guy who, drunk and full
of lip-curled swagger, had loudly cursed
my quoting Ginsberg's poems of love
to an arc of puzzled co-eds.
Of course, I didn't just turn around
and clock him. I tried to reason first,
persuade him to my point of view
that Ginsberg wrote great poems and pounds
of fluff, but that the fluff cannot
muffle all the sweetness, or all
the charged and crazy posturing
and fresh iconoclastic yelping
and magnificent confounding of
the public and the private realms,
and then I whacked him. Of course I was
a fool, and that dyspeptic guy
did not deserve a fool's reproach.
I'd forgotten all about that night
until the woman phoned to mark
from half a continent away
that she recalls a night I fought,
on the porch of a house I would
not recognize these days, about
a man who set his life against
such childishness and schoolboy pride.

It was an ugly little fight
that others wisely stopped before
we really hurt our drunken selves,
and which of us was judged, by all
who'd witnessed our brief dance, the bigger
ass I cannot know and don't much care.
The fool I am forgives the fool
I was, and hopes the guy I punched
can say the same. Though both of us
may feel small consolation in
the fact that our grotesque display
is now odd theater in the mind
of one recalling how a man,
in art, had married art and life
as no one ever will again.

The Comfort Inn

In memory of the poet Lynda Hull

A long-gone friend phoned me up;
her dear voice was a day's small joy
until she paused, breathed deep, and said
that you were killed the other night
on a highway blurred and slicked by snow.

When the phone rang, when our friend's
voice surprised then stunned me, Lynda,
into thoughts of you and David,
I'd been striding, literally,
out the door for spring vacation.
I kept my turmoil to myself;
plans were set and the weather fine.

It was at the Comfort Inn in Gulfport
that this contrivance of talking
to the dead became a rank necessity.

Lynda, there was a light the curtain
couldn't dampen; it seeped through every
pleat and pore, and no matter how still
I lay, it would not let me sleep.
Ema and Dominika breathed
in the farther bed and were not
bothered, but I couldn't turn
or cover my eyes with sheets
or pillow to keep the shine away.
I felt the walls for a switch, then
called the desk. A terse woman said
all the lights were automatic
so could not be switched on or off,
then volunteered that no one else
had ever complained. My anger flared.
I dressed swiftly and stomped downstairs.

She sat curled in a chair watching
TV; her eyes blue and blood-veined,
her hair dirty blond, she seemed someone
who'd wear a hidden tattoo.
I yelled at her about money,
about the power it granted me
over lights and over her.
Outside, a steady breeze jiggled
the plate glass and aluminum frame
of the front door on which a sign
announced that all the rooms were filled.
She was not as frail as you,
as small, and from what she stammered
she was neither smart nor agile,
but after she screamed back at me,
in that moment of glaring silence,
I saw the vague brutalities
her life had absorbed, and I felt
her cheerless youth unraveling
through a dozen jobs in a dozen
motels, bars, and convenience stores
into a cheerless middle age,
and I knew you were her poet,
Lynda, her voice, her dignity,
and I walked out to the glowing pool,
the eerie water lit from beneath,
and filled with shame and sorrow.

Then I lay again in unkillable light,
that vexing beacon to parked cars,
and wept for you, Lynda, and for
that young woman in the lobby
who will never read your poems,
and so will never know that she is blessed
there, at least a little, in your voice.

IV
Wind in the Chimney

The Letters

She's shouting at my face that her room
is wretchedly inadequate in terms
of size and window-space and furnishing
and that I'm responsible for this
tragedy and she'll have my head, or worse,
if at this very second I will fail
to move her to another room with big
bright windows, a softer bed, and of course
she will not share her space with anyone.

I know she has not slept in thirty hours,
and just the bus ride from the airport is
enough to trigger culture shock, and though
I want to shake her like a dog a sock
I smile and promise I will move her to
another room, then drag her baggage down
the hall, obsequious, burning to please.

She has arrived, from the United States,
in Prague to study writing for a month,
and she already wishes she'd not come.
In her fifties, fairly well off, or spoiled
by plenty from my point of view as one
who must insure she gets her money's worth,
she is that kind of American harpy
who terrorizes waiters, salesmen, all
working stiffs who haunt the world of commerce.

And when, just minutes after she has moved
to what's, by standards of this dorm, a penthouse,
I see her trotting, literally, up the hall
again towards me, I swallow, groan and wince
then brace for dead bugs on the window sill,
used condoms hanging from the shower rod,
or rats fucking loudly in the closet,

but she is waving pages in the air
and, halting, breathless, wild–eyed, sputters that
she needs translations of these letters, do
I know of anyone who at this hour
will translate them, for she has come to Prague
to see where family lived before the war,
where uncles, aunts, and cousins made their homes,
where her mother's father owned great buildings
he himself designed, and where now no one
of her blood remains, no one, and only these
old letters, yellowed, brittle, in a tongue
she recalls the music of but cannot speak,
remain as testimony of their lives.

Meluzina

And when she thrusts her baby at my eyes
and when her filthy five-year-old looks up
at my unease and pleads as if in prayer,
I marvel, frozen by the children's beauty,
at how a frank disdain may wither mercy.

But they're not starving, and I am just a mark.
Their daddy's changing money on the Square,
and older sister servicing fat Germans
in Smichov alleys as the sun goes down,
or so I flash until my censor of
such vicious sentiments can do its work
of changing racist haughtiness to shame.
But baby's eyes are shiny-black and deep,
and I just want to take her in my arms
and run back home, clean her, dress her, feed her.
Her pouty little mouth is valentine,
her ruddy cheeks, on which the sooty air
has lain a film upon the mucus crust,
are pudgy yet bedeviled by deep dimples.
I must give her money or burn in hell.

But I am now in love with this dark child,
and only want to hold and feed her, lift
her out of "poverty and ignorance,"
call her Meluzina, the word in Czech
for what the wind sounds like in chimney shafts,
and raise her as my own; my father self
is weeping for the child, longing to wash
her gently, feed her milk and peaches, lay
her down beside my own sweet little girls,
and sing, horribly but gently, till she sleeps.
I do not have enough to give this child
whose cunning mother hoists her, as though she were
a trophy, something precious not for itself,
but for the victory it represents.

Elegy for Miroslav Holub

You passed just days before you were to speak
your poems to yet another dazzled herd
of culture-drunk Americans in Prague.
I tossed away the page I'd scratched that week,
your formal introduction, a polished lie.

What a sweet and modest man you were, how
patient you would be with us, our ignorance,
how sadly you smiled at questions that
could issue only from the hearts of those
untainted by sophistication, and
how elegantly you left the stage,
like magicians' smoke, or a fading light.

Your poems are parables of wonder, cunning
messages of protest, though some may say
too slick, too safe, too obfuscated by
your need to slip iconoclastic jokes
past droop-eyed censors dreaming of Havana.

Scientist and poet, you harkened back
to prehistoric wisdom in your verse
in which you trained a cold and measuring eye
upon the hulking world of stuff, and all
the spooky nonsense honking from its surface.
Ironic shaman, lover of paradox,
large-hearted singer in a tiny language,
you managed to offend so few your voice
was rarely silenced at a time
when to offend was civic obligation.

But who may judge the deeper needs of one
so gentle and civilized as you, good man,
sweet poet, lover of objective fact?

In Memory of Miroslav Prochazka, Scholar of Czech Literature

A smart little guy in love with his pain,
Franz Kafka made a bride of suffering.
In Prague today one sees in some young faces
exquisite torment of the heart that has,
it seems, no mortal object but itself.
Skinny goy Kafkas stare from trams and make
in sad reveries lives fashioned of sighs.
Prague's wan saint of odd angles and paradox,
of father haters everywhere and funk
of youth, still lives in footfalls down back streets
of Old Town at night, when men shuffle from pubs,
neither singing nor cursing, toward sleeping wives.

Late that June we argued in your office
about our jobs and your remuneration.
I stomped away certain my point of view
prevailed, and that our little global venture,
in which Americans soak up your culture
for a month, would flourish in spite of you.

Aficionado of a small republic's
grand tradition, seven years free to write
about the "unofficial" genius of
the old regime: those who stayed and suffered,
those who fled. You seemed in perfect conflict
with yourself, equally loving and resenting
America and things American,
and so it is from your good life I learn
the colonized would rout the colonizers,
except that they become, in part, the things
they hate in those who live to leech quick fortunes,
or live to search the lives of others for
some sparkling meaning lacking in their own.

Somewhere in Prague a girl is scribbling on
a pad, or daydreaming out a window.
She will, perhaps, someday embody all
her generation feels about itself.
Perhaps she'll suffer for her art, and just
as likely she'll exult, as Kafka did,
in how, in art, the selfish making of it,
all our sorrows blossom into grotesque joy.
She is not diminished by your death.
She will be the monster your life's work feeds.

Libuse

Before bright Charles the Fourth mandated both
the Castle and St. Vitus, and had dreamed
so much of Prague that is still glorious,
a little patch above what's now Prague 4
was home to legendary kings and queens,
and one folktale, from when the Slavs were tribes
just through with wandering and hunkered down
upon this ridge above the Vltava,
recalls a full-scale war between the men
and women that the women won, before
they were vanquished utterly unto this day.

My daughters walk with me through Vysehrad,
the three-year old waddling from potential harm
to near-disaster, touching everything,
or trying to; the nine-year old just talks
unceasingly, firing questions faster than
I can respond, not waiting for an answer
before assaulting with another one.
As a younger man I could not know that some
day I would relish such a harried joy
as strolling hand-in-hand with little girls.

What may a man in good faith dream for them?
I dream they rise above their bodies' codes
as every man and woman must who's not
insane or drifting in a gray despair,
and so refuse all urges to submit
their lives to promises of tenderness,
even as each seeks her fount of tenderness.
I dream they find that power over life
which is firm tethering to an endless task.
I dream they live as though each waking hour
were prayer to nothing but their love of life,
and to that end are kind to all who wish
them well, but swift to strike at enemies,
at least such ones as do them covert harm.
I dream for them long lives of sweet resistance,
and as we pause at the feet of Libuse,
the prescient heroine of ancient Prague,
the small one squeals, then pulls away and runs
to climb the statue, and the older one
just wants to know if a woman chiseled it.

Germans in the Pool

Signs state, quite clearly, in Czech and German both,
that diving is forbidden, and tossing balls
verboten, too, and so they seem uncouth

at least, as rubber bubbles smack the walls
to dribble back, and beefy bodies plunk
and souse, indifferent to our pleading calls

that they should heed the signs and cease to dunk
themselves from pool's edge, missing children's heads
by inches, changing childish fun to funk.

But when I've finally had enough and said,
"Why can't you goddamned Germans do what's right?"
so loudly the pool grows quiet, fills with dread,

I'm sickly certain I've just picked a fight
with fourteen Huns whose bodies' total weight
of sixteen hundred kilos will soon light

upon my face and chest to seal my fate,
or crush it flat, and my vacation weeks
of snowy slopes and mountain air deflate.

I stare through soot-stained glass at creamy peaks
and watch the tiny skiers weaving down.
The heated breath inside this greenhouse reeks

of chlorine, and from the quiet tension sound
the chugging hisses of electric pumps
that suck and filter pissed-in water round

and through a chambered cycle, and then dump
it back for healthy contact with our skin.
My German brothers rest their German rumps

against the pool wall, cross their arms, begin
to weigh their options, maybe feel the need
to pry their horseplay from their fathers' sins.

Inciting all to make those Nazis bleed,
the propaganda flicks I grew up on
still work their magic for this goofy breed

of bad boys frolicking, by bargains drawn
to where their fathers' fathers once impressed
a wicked will, and now this cheerful spawn

seem merely ancient wickedness at rest.
They smirk and wave me off and shoot me stares,
as if this were my problem more than theirs.

An American Lawyer in Olomouc

For Bill Tete

An American lawyer who is decent
truly, and therefore even in the tethering
of "American" and "lawyer" seems to make
of the shame of both an honorable life,
leads us on a tour of Olomouc, where we
have come by car to visit for the day.

My Prague-centrist wife finds the city quaint,
a place she has visited but once before
though nothing in this country is too far
to reach in half a day except on foot
(and even hoofing one can make a dent
in any map that's faithful to proportion).

Five years ago our friend did Fulbright time
here at the law school lecturing in English,
though he is focused now on studying
this language I can only understand
in tiny fits of comprehension, and speak
so poorly my fluent darling eight-year old
winces when I stutter through a phrase
so rife with errors meaning chokes and dies.
Our lawyer friend's bad accent notwithstanding,
he is a good and faithful student of
this language and the history of these folks,
these dour Moravians whom he has come
to love as inexplicably as deeply.

I'll leave him to his reasons, though when he says
he feels at home here more than in New Orleans
I'm mildly shocked, for I have heard him speak
with casual humor and respect of men
who lived Louisiana fast and loose—
his father, father's father, and their brothers
who lived the good lives that a little money

and connections brought to white men of that time.
Most are now interred in St. Louis Three
at the end of Esplanade, and when he leads
us from the tram across the street and through
the gate of Olomouc's best cemetery,
I wonder what it is here justifies
this trek past rows of Slavic names, a few
ill-kept and German, and, even, through a hedge,
a clutch of Jewish graves and tombs that kids
are weeding, tending to, "because the German
government is paying to make this part
as nice as it had been before the war,"
one tells us, as she hacks the vines from Hebrew
script on marble, in Slovak even I
can understand, and so I place a stone
upon a poet's grave we happen past
and cross back through the hedge that hides the Jews
and all the good that German money does.

But now our lawyer friend insists we view
the heart of Olomouc's cemetery,
the very center, that is graveled over,
where a monument six meters tall, red star
upon its pinnacle, commemorates
the Soviets who perished wrenching back
this little city from a Nazi force.
They'd come from liberating Auschwitz, to die
in Olomouc in Nineteen Forty-five.

Grouped by rank, the red star atop each stone,
the thirty graves, or so, that I can see—
some others may be tucked away among
the foliage that's manicured and wild

by turns throughout this oddly plotted place—
have pictures of the soldiers lacquered on
the marble, and who they were and when they died
recorded in Cyrillic script. And on
the ground, in the dull white gravel, someone
has traced a star before the monument,
and written "Moscow" in Cyrillic, and as
we wonder at two British graves among
the Russian ones—our friend is sure their markers
have been here since the Brits' interment, though
my wife is sure they've been here only since
the Velvet Revolution, nine years ago—
I smudge a corner of the gravel star
idly with my shoe, then stop, and feel ashamed,
and try to trace it back, but the point is lost.

What we call home is where we choose to die,
or where, dying, we long with fading hearts
to be; our "cert," our tiny devil girl
who's not yet two and whom we've brought to give
our eight-year-old some time with their babicka,
in the scant seconds I let her waddle off,
shatters a green vase of withered blooms,
is miraculously uncut, and pads
away grunting and cooing among the stones.

Tick

A rare occasion our child was not with one
or both of us, we poked through Prague's clogged streets,
domestic errands in our wake, until
the gray Mercedes surged to lunge ahead
of our little red Fiesta, even though
the bottleneck of traffic halted all.
He imperiled us, almost caused a crash,
simply to gain a length's advantage
in the stalled and stinky summer queue of cars.
Dominika slammed her palm into the horn,
showed her teeth, and I was delighted by
her anger, so scooted out the door and flipped
the bastard off with both my middle fingers.
He leaped out scowling and ready for a fight.
He tried to kick me but I blocked it, boxed
his ear and plucked his forehead, pointed at
his car as if he were a little boy
and I his daddy pointing to his room.
A swarthy fellow wearing pricey clothes,
he seemed a Slavic low-rent Casanova.
But when he popped his trunk and pulled out black
and shiny rags he peeled from metal, then
snatched a cartridge and jammed it in and spun
I saw his fully automatic thing
for killing, his Uzi or whatever god
damned thing it was, an automatic weapon,
the kind that sprays its bullets so that aiming's
not an issue, and suddenly I thought
that here at last I'd done it, I'd finally pissed
off someone with a weapon and the will
to use it, after years of mouthing off
in biker bars and leaning on my horn

in New Orleans—where once good men got lynched
for less—after a youth of not caring whom
I angered and well into middle life
unscarred, unbowed, in Prague, in summer, I
would die of road rage, but thought the noble thing
to do would be to run aslant, drawing fire
away from Dominika, and in that tick
it took to turn I saw her raising Ema
alone, and Ema living fatherless,
and Ema's face, and I heard Ema's voice
and clearly the greasy pimp didn't shoot
or I'd not be writing this, but that tick,
that tiny jagged piece of time, got packed
with self-recrimination, boundless love
for a woman and a child, for every friend
and minor enemy my life had vexed,
and even a little humor, for as
I turned I thought oh God I'm wearing drawers
with three small holes around the baggy crotch,
and every mother's admonition honked
inside my head, as then I tripped and fell.

Prague Winter:
Sonnet Stanzas for My Daughter

1.

My baby wants to know if she is more
American than Czech, to which I say
that she is what has never been before,
a perfect blending of the two, the play
of what is best in both in one good girl.
At this she wonders why the kids at school
call her "Americanka," even curl
their lips in funny smiles to say it. "Fools,"
I blurt, but then sigh, "no, not fools, just kids."
They learn at supper tables that contempt
is antidote to envy, that it rids
the small, green heart of what one dares not tempt
from shadows of the self-sought self: the sense
that all one's life is but a sad defense.

2.

But she who speaks two worlds with one quick tongue,
who learns in Czech but rants and drifts at home
in English so American its foam
of effervescence is a tide that's sung
by Whitman no more so than dim-wit jock,
my dreamy girl just wants to be their friend.
For this she must, I tell her, learn to bend
the arc of her lone flight and join the flock,
but that the trick of knowing happiness
is to find the perfect distance from us all,
a quantity that changes every day.
Delight, my dear, in your sweet otherness.
True friends you'll know when years compel you trawl
the dark tides of your mind, where wishes sway.

3.

The issue, finally, daughter, may well be
those princesses of old Bohemia,
the ones you read about and can't but see
in movies, black-and-white, from when to be a
female was to be princess of the State,
a beaming worker for the Greater Good.
In each it is the pouty royal's fate
to learn that peasants' wisdom is what should
determine life of kingdom, but of course
the message is a muddle of traditions,
as finally princess learns to feel remorse
for being princess, marries prince, bears sons.
May power over love be your true art,
when someday you are queen of someone's heart.

4.

Love child of the Velvet Revolution,
residual passion of that passion play
in which no god of flesh was made to pay
for sins, just little men whose jobs were done,
nine months into the sweet and brutal change
your life appeared, I held you in my arms,
and nothing from that moment would bring harms
to you except that through my rage it range.
And now, but ten years after all those joys
of shucking off absurdity of brutes,
and fashioning a gentler circumstance
by which the commerce of our lives alloys
our baser aspects with what nature mutes,
in fools, you are the shine of second chance.

5.

My smart and drifty child, sometimes you stare
so vacantly I worry where you are,
and wonder what enchantment flew you there,
and by what charm you stalk the most bizarre
scenarios you breathlessly relate
upon emerging from your reverie.
Within the worlds you dream all threats abate
and Chance rewards each act of decency.
Yet over this glorious and wacky place
at Europe's heart a sorrow hangs like smoke.
A sixty-year-old evil leaves its trace
even on such dreams as innocents evoke.
So self-consumed yet filled with empathy,
you're poised to bear your share of history.

V
Feuilletons

The Art of Teaching

is an unpaved road to a wild place in summer, at the end of which a thicket holds a nest of ugly hatchlings. Crouch and watch the parents return again and again with pieces of death; no matter how often they fling themselves against the hot air and return with bits in their mouths for the mouths they were driven to coax into the heat and wind of the world, it is not enough, or so the little ones seem to say by all their racket, all their bobbing in the fetid straw, that little dance of the weak-necked insatiable, that little dance of a hunger whose purpose, they feel even if they do not know, is flight. And yet what purpose

of such purpose? And of that, what purpose? Ask the worm, the beetle, the tiny lizard, all that are vexed by flight. But do not ask the bird of prey, or that idiot in the middle of nowhere crouching in the heat.

The Tennessee Williams Literary Festival

is an annual four-day event to which I am rarely invited. Once, I was
asked by the organizers to read my poems with four other people
who read their poems before and after me, and we were all introduced
by Alice Quinn, who was paid quite well to fly down to New Orleans
and introduce us, though we ourselves received little remuneration.
Our compensation by the organizers for performing our poems was
to be introduced by Alice Quinn, who did so with all the understated
class and elegance one expects from an editor for *The New Yorker*. In
fact, Alice Quinn's introductions of us were much better than most of
the poems we subsequently read to that audience, more understated,
more eloquent, more tactful, tasteful, and, mercifully, more brief.

My Best Lesbian Friend

let's me off the hook again and again, shaking her head and tisking, but knowing that I try, really try, not to be a dog. Her patience is a stream whose source is far, far away, and whose mouth opens out into an alluvial fan composed of my indiscretions.

I would give her the world if it were mine to give, for she would know what to do with it, how to fix it, with grace. I would hand it over not because she is a lesbian, and not because she is my friend, and certainly not because she is my best lesbian friend, but because

once from a window I watched her step from a cab into a wad of fresh feces, and, after tossing, with no malice, a bill on the seat beside the driver, then pressing the door shut, she scraped the mess from her shoe on the curb, then, standing straight and peering down, rubbed that sole on the moist grass, and as she did there was no disgust in her face, only resolve verging on joy.

Movie Critics

are of three basic types: failed novelists, failed poets, and lovers of cinema. It is she or he who loves cinema whose judgments I least trust. When I am about to put my good money down for two hours of just sitting and staring, I will reflect first upon the judgments of a failed novelist regarding a new movie from Hollywood, or, God help us, Paris,

for all novelists are failures inasmuch as none achieves godhood, at least not in the sense that a movie director or producer or even a best boy achieves a kind of fleeting deification as the credits roll, and some people sit and watch all the names scroll past, knowing they will recall nothing of what is written there, but feeling a kind of duty, and basking in the grudging admiration of those who (feeling a little guilty, but defiantly so) have risen to leave. Our movie critic is that fellow in the last row whose third book got remaindered almost as quickly as his second (though it had returned to the winning themes of his first), mumbling into a cassette recorder, wiping the salt and grease from his other hand on the empty seat beside him.

Pariah

Until you piss off an entire community, you may know nothing of bliss. For bliss, as I conceive it here, is freedom from the obligations of tact.

Colleague A nods as he passes. "You haven't published in decades," I say with a smile, nodding back. Colleague B gives a little wave with her free hand as she reaches for her mail. "Still sleeping with the dean?" I ask, rubbing the air between us with my palm. Our secretary, who knows better by now than to lift her eyes from the nonsense on her desk when I pass, just stiffens. Our chairman, though, cannot help himself. He rushes into the hall when the taps on my shoes clatter past his office. "You are evil!" he shouts. "We all hate you!"

to which I do not reply, because I am headed for the Faculty Lounge where I must post fake snapshots, on the corkboard above the microwave, of his wife engaging our new medievalist, naked.

The Art of Revenge

is irony sticking it to ire, "it" being flaccid yet somehow functional. Legend has it a whole family committed suicide because of some poetry that Archilocus inflicted upon them; the father, the story goes, had promised a daughter to that mercenary, that soldier-poet, but reneged. I imagine the poet aghast, overwhelmed by the news of the effect of his verse upon those who had slighted him, indeed inspired him (in the archaic sense) by their slight. I imagine him sad, but not weeping. I imagine

him a homely man, a tough guy who's seen a lot and believes in nothing, a real prick but with a heart, and an unabashed longing for symmetry.

If I Were a Jew

I would be very worried, all the time, for I am reading Paul Johnson's
A History of the Jews, and neither Paul Johnson nor I is a Jew though
we are filled with empathy, he being erudite and brilliant, I drinking
in that brilliant erudition. Of course, if I were a Jew, I would not
require a goy, even a brilliant if conservative one like Paul Johnson,
to empathize with me; such empathy as I feel is not born of necessity.
For at the heart of the subjunctive mood

lies the foundation of Jericho, the rank breath of God on stone,
and the afterthought of a rabbi, sitting in his study, gazing over his
glasses at the far wall, his finger in the air, mumbling the clincher in
an argument with his dead father or Maimonides. Oh, if I could be
Anne Frank's golem, deployed across the dangerous boulevards of
night raids, I would be an agent of harm to all that would harm her.
Fashioned from the clay of any great river, I would roam, the essence
of vigilance, the Book of Life crammed in my mouth, the dream of
peace a fog blowing off of that river.

The Gossip

If I were not myself so vulnerable, I would delight in her sickness, this
compulsion to secrete information best left stacked in the Warehouse
of Infamy and Vacuous Chatter. And she must have a subject, so hauls
from the recent past sordid news, and no one known to ourselves
present but themselves is not sullied.

A's German wife is consorting with a Saudi grad student, and A's
Polish mistress gave all three herpes. B's gay husband has found Jesus,
a morose hunk from Houston. C's had work done. D's tubes are tied,
as are the hands of her lover who likes it rough. E, poor E . . .

When she is finished so is the evening, and I am exhausted, burdened
with knowledge of the private lives of friends, unconfirmed bits sifted
from the dross of our sorrows, blessings, wild imaginings,

rather like the stuff of myths and holy texts, with the sole difference of
intention.

The Cumulative Weight of Despair

is buoyant in direct proportion to one's long view of history, history
being what has happened to everyone you don't know, a long view
contrasting with a short one only in terms of empathy (I suppose this
was Yeats' odd point in "Lapis Lazuli"). For example, in the spring of
1969 I toured the "Atrocity Museum" in Nagasaki, and one of the
other students, gazing at a black-and-white photo of a girl whose
skin was peeling from her chest and arms and face, stage-whispered,
"French-fried Japs!" His was a long view of recent history. In Terezin
in 1997, a little man, our tour guide, led twenty of us into a stall and
closed the door. Through a slot, he informed us that exactly as many
people got crammed into that precise space and were kept there for
days, rotating onto the narrow cot for a few moments' rest, relieving
their bladders and bowels squatting where they stood, body to body.
He was gifting us a short view of history, on whose horizon the
cumulative weight of despair may never stop sinking.

Rich People Slumming in Academe

should not be poohpoohed just because their inherited wealth means that to eat they do not require employment. They bring to the classroom points of view untainted by necessity. They wear wealth like an exquisite undergarment, the kind we perceive though it is hidden, because they who feel wealth on their skin bear all that is motley as though it were only costume. Some put their paychecks into trusts that they give back to the institutions upon retirement as though it had all been just a tasteful joke. Some profess

at universities where the children of their peers matriculate, though some take jobs at institutions established for the first generations that are not cycled into coal mines or factories, onto fishing boats or trains, and serve there as the bootstraps by which such may improve themselves. They are angels, brought down by that American imperative against ostentatious display of class difference, humble agents of divine assistance, mocking precisely that which their progenitors haunt, the vast contingencies of leisure from which any soul, once lost among those innumerable interlocking chambers, may never return as anything but forlorn.

Blessings on commerce of the mind, and all, all who seek its community, especially its slums.

As When Someone with Long Beautiful Hair Turns Around

and it's an ugly little guy with a handlebar mustache, so is our daily passage tethered to disappointment by a thread of hope, which is to say it's the wise man who trains himself to regard hopelessly, a wise woman likewise, and a lucky man or woman who finds such a woman or man, and a wise woman or man who seeks such a man or woman, whether she or he is much to look at, or not.

George W. Bush Was Very Nice to Me

as Bacchus rolled down St. Charles, and I chatted with him about
politics, local and national, especially the eleven-fingered idiot
running against David Duke for the Republican nomination for
Fuhrer of the Suburbs. I told him flat out I hate the Republican Party
and still he was nice to me, stood next to me, in the back of the ten-
deep crowd that yelled for trinkets, and chatted for several minutes as
though he really liked me, and didn't mind at all that I'd ripped a fine
white string of beads from his grasp when he grabbed it from the air
at the same time as I. As we chatted about Duke and New Orleans
apartheid, about my having recently lived in the French Quarter and
about how the trees on St. Charles seem for months after Carnival–
indeed on some stretches all year round–like bearers of many-colored
fruit from where the bead strands get caught in the branches, I knew
I would one day write about meeting the president's goofy son, a nice
guy, which is to say someone you shouldn't mind standing around
shooting the breeze with on a pleasant spring night in New Orleans,
though not someone you'd want to be cooped up with on a long
drive, say, from El Paso to San Antonio, or certainly not from one
paradigm to another.

Each Customer Is an Odious Task

to the women who work the counters of Prague's neighborhood
grocery stores, and I am odious beyond contempt for I am an
American, which is to say my appetites are large, my wallet deep, and
my Czech hilarious except that it is tragic what I do to their mother
tongue. They are puffy beyond menopause, beyond romance, beyond
judgment; they seem a force of nature

in the sense that Marx conceived "the proletariat" a force of nature,
and thereby condemned it to surly accommodation, a moody
efficiency meant only to move you along. There is no such thing as
service with a smile

among those who conceive themselves a ruling class consigned to
an ash heap, not that before the "Velvet Revolution" there was any
sunshine in their demeanors, though

then at least there was an ideological basis, a philosophical justification
to their condescension.

Now, the whole process is merely elemental: You require what is in
their charge, and after an exchange approximating biology, you are
flushed from their aisles

onto the gorgeous streets of an ancient city, all that you require for
a pleasant meal in a plastic sack, all that you require of "community"
contained in the unearthly imperative that it does its job and leaves
you alone.

In America They Would Get Shot

on any freeway, but especially in the South, especially on I10. The left lane, no one should have to argue, is primarily for passing, but there are circumstances when, especially if one deigns to cruise ten miles-an-hour over the limit, it's okay to camp in the left lane, for example when there is a long line of trucks in the right lane and the grade is slightly up. But in Europe, and I don't mean just on the Autobahn, under such circumstances, even a Skoda will come up within inches of your bumper and just hang there for kilometers, waiting for you to do the right thing and swing behind a blue truck from Slovakia belching a wholly unregulated filth. Sometimes Euroman will flash his lights, as though imperiling your life and the lives of your family by riding your bumper at eighty miles-an-hour hadn't made the point, and in the rearview mirror you can see it's some chinless geek who's probably good with numbers, that he's not at all worked up, that this is simply common practice, that you're the asshole, by the standards of the culture, for not sliding over, but

you think of all the bubbas on the highways between New Orleans and Tallahassee, how you know better than to flip them off on I10, how all of them have pistols under the seats of their solid rides, their big, insatiable American cars, and you think for a second how much more courteous, by your standards, European highways would be if country-bumpkin Hungarians and Poles carried handguns, but then you can't believe such an incredibly stupid thought just raced through your mind, right up to the tailpipe of your liberalism, which stays put, but more out of fear than conviction.

The Slovaks

are employed by my mother-in-law's companion, who has
subcontracted to refurbish and landscape the courtyard of this
building owned by my wife and her brother. I warned limply against
hiring, sort of, within the family, but my mother-in-law's companion,
seventy-two and retired, has discovered the joys of private enterprise
after a pre-Revolution career of diddling at the city's waterworks, and
put in a bid ridiculously lower than the others. They arrive

at six and work until six, and are performing, by all indications, in
spectacular fashion. The wall rises; shrubs proliferate; each day's mess
gets cleaned up. Every couple of hours my wife gazes down from
five stories at their efforts and speaks satisfaction. She is as surprised
as I that her mother's companion's workers are actually performing,
making progress. She notes that they are not drinking liters and liters
of beer while they work as Czech laborers do; in fact, they seem not
to be drinking at all. They work almost noiselessly, eerily so, and seem
so grateful when she gives them a little extra money on the side that
our hearts break a little. When I opine that they are a credit to their
nation, my wife knows I am joking, gets the silly spiral of associations
back to racism in America, but doesn't smile, just nods agreement,
for this dedication to task and the admiration it evokes is something
between people whose differences are mysterious to everyone but
themselves.

Ordinary Czechs Singing on TV

is a big hit here. It's nothing like *Ted Mack's Amateur Hour* or *Star Search*; these people have absolutely no talent. Indeed, most of them are wretched singers and yet will stand before the cameras and studio audience and wail popular songs with more passion and conviction than should ever be encouraged. There is an actual orchestra, and the insinuation of rehearsals, and these dour Slavs work the microphone like sexy beasts, though most are homely. The show's a hit, so it's karaoke on a national scale, though they're all sober and no one's egging them on. They sing for keeps because

they seem to know how terrible they are, that they will never be allowed to do this again, so most of their performances seem less to do with delusion than despair. The cafeteria worker from Olomouc, a hefty nineteen-year-old with bowl-cut greasy hair and zits, was my favorite. She belted out a popular Czech song about shy love, and seemed to mean every word. She was two beats behind a studio orchestra that's used to changing tempo mid-phrase, and as flat as her own expectations, but she rose to the moment, spiritually, I'll say, yes, spiritually she rose to the occasion. She didn't just sing; she performed, and her performance embodied shy love defying its own nature, yes, she was shy love defying its own nature in a tiny nation at the core of Europe, in a language hardly anyone beyond the borders can understand, except Slovaks (and Poles, a little). She made a fool of herself in front of her nation, and would never be able to hide, to disappear. She traveled from Olomouc to Prague, the Big City, and became shy love defying its own nature for two minutes before half the population of her nation and will probably regret having done so for the rest of her life, which I hope is long and remains on its own terms heroic.

There's No Tragic Weather Here

most years, and when the "worst floods in a century" tore over the placid Bohemian and Moravian landscapes, the damage, in Old World terms, was fleeting. When I was a child we got chased by a "big-ass tornado," as my father called the thing, though that danger was nothing personal, I knew even then we'd not been targeted, and we celebrated a little as it seemed that our car outran the dirty funnel, though its chasing us, following, that is, the same path as the highway we were on, was probably an illusion, a trick of two moving objects within angles of sifted light.

It rained from sun to sun last night in Prague. I thought of storms and scourges in the New World, each season's legions of hurricanes, the god-like towers of gray winds that drop upon the plains, fires that scour vast swaths of land, the tremors presaging disasters beyond imagining. I lay in the flashed dark as patrician thunder barely quivered the window glass, and recalled the thumping thrill of Gulf Coast torrents, my shameful fear of summer lightning, and considered, only rapidly to reject, all obvious analogies to history and destiny in which ironic reversal accounts for the horrors of the Old World, the vacuous hope of the New. I lay in shadows and listened to the sleeping breath of my Old World wife and that of our daughters in adjacent rooms, and fancied Lear, that fond old man, cozying into his dotage in the New World, rocking and staring out over the darkening Gulf, a mutt at his feet, chanting the name of a storm that is coming.

The Liberal Arts

are where you bring a lot of articulate people together to compete for relatively meager resources. It is the rubric under which the chasm between information and knowledge contains at its bottom the bone yard of Youthful Exuberance, and where the high-minded and petty dance slow, close and dirty through the crumbling stacks of the Library of Babel. It is where the dreamy brothers and sisters of scientists and technicians are kept out of the flight path of real thought, a kind of holding tank with soft walls and benches, or a leper colony with soft walls and benches, even gardens and fountains. It is where you scoot off the otherwise uneducable young to, and where all others must pass quickly as through the section of a natural museum that is long aisles of rocks under glass. And is not the "canon" just rocks under glass? Objects of dispassionate scrutiny, though also potential, if primitive, weapons?

The Super Rich Are an Oppressed Minority

that has no choice but to defend itself against the machinations of hoi
polloi, the kidnapping and lying, the acts of theft and destruction and
gross bad faith, but especially the inept service and envious glances.
"The eye of a needle," scholars tell us, was a portal into the city large
enough for a man on his donkey to pass through. So may all rich men
and women and their progeny pass in single file from the Free Market
Wastes into the Heavenly City, where commerce is unregulated
and taxes perfunctory and meager. May those of us unconnected,
unmotivated, disinherited, unfocused and clueless, those of us lacking
talent and drive, we who were born with plastic spoons in our
mouths, learn to express compassion for all who possess the means of
production and therefore also the will to fuck us. And when they do,
let us only shyly insist that they also hold us close and kiss us.

Two Fellows Only a Little Swarthier Than I

passed as I checked my mailbox; they seemed furtive as they left the
building, and I followed them out wondering who they were, and
asked them, in English, on a hunch, if they lived in the building even
though I knew they didn't. The taller one said they were visiting a
tenant whose name he then mangled. I smiled and said, "Fine," and
walked on, noting their dress down to their shoes, considering how I
would describe their faces. For I was certain

they were plotting to blow something up, Radio Free Europe or
the Palace of Culture which is anything but, but which is huge and
equipped to accommodate great meetings of the IMF, NATO, and
other symbols of Western oppression. I was certain, too, that they
were just two guys from Morocco or Yemen trying to make a living,
in town on some business deal that would bring finely embroidered
carpets to Central Europe, two guys who learned some English
because you've just got to if you want to slip out of Morocco or
Yemen even for a little while, and who have to put up with this shit
constantly, the hard looks of suspicion, the hateful fear in the eyes of
those who stare. Who wouldn't be furtive?

Who doesn't see devils where he's seen as one? And if, as the saying
goes, it is details that malevolence inhabits, it is by generalities it
transports itself from fact to fact to fact.

A Brief History of Your Conception

(Composed on the day of your birth)

I recall the commercial for Radio Free Europe when I was ten,
residing in public housing in Norfolk, Virginia. Checkoso-
whatchamacallit sounded like a terrible place to live, worse, even, than
Newport News. The word looked like a disease, and being behind the
"iron curtain" had to resemble being in an "iron lung."

When I was fifteen I heard on Armed Forces Radio that Russia had
invaded it. My adoptive father, really my uncle by marriage, was
sweeping mines off the coast of Vietnam, and I was a pain in the
ass of Sasebo, Japan. Cherry blossoms littered my path to the bars
downtown.

Last summer I met your mother. She was beautiful and funny and
very bright. So, though married to another, I contrived to go to
the country whose name looked like a disease, to the city Russia
had quieted. This past autumn, I stood in crowds of people taking
themselves just seriously enough.

There are no pure motives even unto death; my beckoning you forth
from ignorance was that I might pardon myself, but you are more
potent than forgiveness. The day preceding the night you were
conceived I passed through a gauntlet of saints, kings and angels on
Charles Bridge; their stone eyes seemed curious, or malicious, and
their heroic postures but propaganda for paradise. Tourist of a gentle
revolution, I was as taken with the dashed-off slogans taped to subway
columns as with such permanent emblems of "national identity."

That night, between the sheets of energy and artifice, you were
conceived. My darling, my tiny Bohemian, someday we will toss gray
Czech bread to the filthy swans of the Vltava, and you will laugh at
my bad Czech grammar. Or a thousand sorrows will darken the sky
with slow wings, and I will write your name in salt. Ema, the world is
enormous. Pity it, and love accordingly.

Notes:

My Czech family and friends will notice immediately that I have left all diacritics off of Czech words and names. I have done this because it is easier to omit them than apply them appropriately, but also because I know that anyone even with a passing familiarity with the Czech language (a relation, alas, I can barely claim after over a decade in proximity to it), will know precisely where in this book the letter "c" should be pronounced "ch," as in "chair," and "s" pronounced "sh," as in "ship" (I have avoided all Czech words in which occur the "r," topped by a little "v," that is pronounced like . . . well, a weary "j" that has put its arm around the heaving shoulders of a grieving "r"), though only a Czech truly understands, in her Bohemian and/or Moravian bones, when and why a long "e" in English becomes in Czech a "y," "i," or "e," and with an accent or not (I have of course left off all accents denoting long vowels; the distinction is lost on all ears not tuned to Czech). Suffice it here to say that the "J" in Jakes is like a "Y" in English, and the "s" like "sh"; it is a two-syllable word with the accent on the first syllable (In Czech, the accent is always on the first syllable). The "s" in Srut, Smid, Skoda, and Vysehrad is also "sh." The "c" in Dubcek is the English "ch," as it is in Obcanske, kyticka, cert, Americanka and babicka.

"The Bridge of Intellectuals"
 A few kilometers outside of Prague, on the main highway going south along the Vltava, is a nondescript railway bridge that was built, it is said, by artists, musicians, writers, scholars, and philosophers, who were compelled by the newly installed Communist authorities after the "Elegant Coup" of 1948 to labor at this public works project as a regimen of "rehabilitation." It is commonly referred to as the Bridge of Intellectuals. This poem, besides being a tribute to Czech artists of that time in terms of subject, is also a tribute to certain American poets in terms of style.

"Socialism with a Human Face"
This phrase was the motto of the Czechoslovak reform movement of 1968, and the sentiment it embodied, the social and cultural blossoming it inspired, called the Prague Spring, precipitated the Soviet invasion of that year and the period of "Normalization" that followed.

Czechoslovakia had one of the world's most vital economies between the Wars; T.G. Masaryk, a philosopher and academic (married to an American), was the patriarch of the Czechoslovak First Republic, and its first president. Alexander Dubcek, a Slovak, was President of Czechoslovakia during the Prague Spring and became a symbol of Czechoslovak humiliation following the invasion. In 1989, on the occasion of one of the Velvet Revolution's (Czechs use this term, but many are also a little embarrassed by it) largest protest rallies, he stood triumphantly with Vaclav Havel on a balcony overlooking Wenceslas Square.

Martin Smid was a math student who was rumored to have been beaten to death by the police during the student protest march of November 17, 1989. The next day, a memorial of candles marked the spot on Narodni trida where it was said he had been killed. It turned out that he'd not been killed, only beaten, but the rumor of his death sparked the first spontaneous protest rally on Wenceslas Square.

Milos Jakes was the hilariously inarticulate (I'm told) boss of the old regime.

"The Book of Complaints"
Pavel Srut, who was not allowed to publish his poetry for over twenty years, is one of the Czech Republic's finest poets.

Through the early '90s, one could stroll among the headstones of the Jewish Cemetery. In response to the huge increase in tourist traffic, the area has been cordoned off in recent years.

The story of how poised and dignified, how noble Czech and Slovak young people were during the Velvet Revolution has not yet been adequately told outside the region. One of the banners waving over the crowds on Wenceslas Square in November of 1989 read in Czech: "WE WHO WERE STUDENTS IN '68 ARE PROUD OF OUR CHILDREN."

"After Frank Zappa's Visit to the Castle"
It seemed like a glorious summit meeting of two master absurdists
when Frank Zappa visited Vaclav Havel in the Castle just months after
the Velvet Revolution. *Weasels Rip My Flesh* is the title of one of the
Mothers of Invention early-'70s albums.

"Saint Roch"
As is generally true of saints, stories vary regarding his supernatural
accomplishments. Suffice it to say that he is associated with the
plague, with tending to plague victims, and therefore with massive
physical suffering and anguish.

"Love Poem for an Enemy"
I wish simply to report here that everyone who has speculated as to
whom this poem refers is absolutely correct.

"Elegy for Robert L. Jones"
Bob Jones ("Honez," the Spanish pronunciation of "Jones," to his
legions of friends) was one of our finest translators of Mexican poetry.
Born and raised in Fresno but a resident of San Diego for more than
twenty years, he was also one of our wisest and most soulful lyric
poets.

"Meluzina"
I wanted to name my first daughter Meluzina (a Czech word that
names the sound the wind makes in the chimney), but Dominika
was horrified by the idea. There is a more or less "official" list of
names available to Czechs (though the Czechs aren't alone in this, just
seemingly more rigid than most other Europeans), each assigned its
"Name Day" on the calendar, from which one may not, according to
powerful convention, stray.

Discrimination against Roma, "Gypsies," in Central Europe, and
particularly in the Czech Republic, is well documented. What is
not so well documented is how easy it is for even the most well-
intentioned European-American to fall victim to the ugly sentiments
of such discrimination, especially given that racism against Gypsies,

though certainly no less pernicious, has a very different historical context and social structure in the Czech lands and the rest of Central Europe than does racism against African-Americans, Native Americans, and other minorities in America.

With the possible exception of the relation of non-Native Americans to Native Americans in some parts of the South-Western U.S., there is no parallel in American society to the relation of non-Gypsy Czechs to Gypsy Czechs (for example, the usual distinction is between "Czech" and "Roma," as though Gypsies were not citizens).

"Elegy for Miroslav Holub"
The case of Holub is but one example of how extremely complex the relation of the artist to the state had been before 1989. Those in the West who celebrated Holub as a dissident were flatly wrong. He was a brilliant, gifted, humane artist, scientist, and citizen of the world, but his relation to the totalitarian authority of the pre-1989 Czechoslovak state was ambiguous, as was true for well over ninety-nine percent of the population. Dissidents were very small in number; there was little or no ambiguity in their response to oppression, and they paid for that clarity.

"In Memory of Miroslav Prochazka, Scholar of Czech Literature"
What indeed is "Czech literature?" Does it, should it, contain German-language literature, and therefore Kafka? The history of Czech nationalism, for better and for worse, underpins all things "Czech," and Kafka, as a German speaker for whom Czech was a second language, but especially as a Jew, I suppose was the ultimate anti-Czech no less so than he was to become, posthumously, the ultimate anti-Citizen of the World. And Kafka is in fact a transcendent figure for Czech intellectuals, a kind of crazy uncle in the attic who knows all the family's secrets. Miroslav Prochazka, an extremely bright and decent man who died much too young, once spoke to me wistfully over beers about the parallels, for Czechs, between Austro-Hungarian, Nazi, Soviet Russian and American cultural hegemony.

"Libuse"
Vysehrad, in now what is Prague 4, lay upon a ridge overlooking
the Vltava. It is where the first Premyslovci kings were ensconced,
though for centuries the rulers shuttled between Vysehrad, south of
the Old and New Towns, and what is now the "Castle" (though not
the one Kafka refers to, oddly enough) that looms famously over the
city on. Libuse (three syllables), whose name has taken different forms
and whose legend is as elastic as that of any hulking figure of national
myth, in all the permutations of her legend predicted the existence of
Prague, and predicted as well its greatness. Though her first prediction
is irrefutable, even many Czechs would agree that history's jury is still
out on the second.

Four five-meter tall statues—two parallel and roughly ten meters apart
facing the other two roughly fifty meters away; they form a rectangle
that frames a lawn at the center of a promenade—guard the Vysehrad
park.

Feuilletons
My "feuilletons" are not prose poems (with the possible exception
of the last, which I composed on the day of my oldest daughter's
birth and at a time when I wasn't familiar with the form, though the
text has indeed slightly transformed over the past twelve years). The
feuilleton is of course a French form of ephemeral journalism, though
before 1989 in Eastern and Central Europe many dissident writers
adapted it to the weightier concerns of "samizdat." My feuilletons are
actually much briefer than those of, say, the great Ludvik Vaculik, who
says a feuilleton should be roughly three typed pages long.